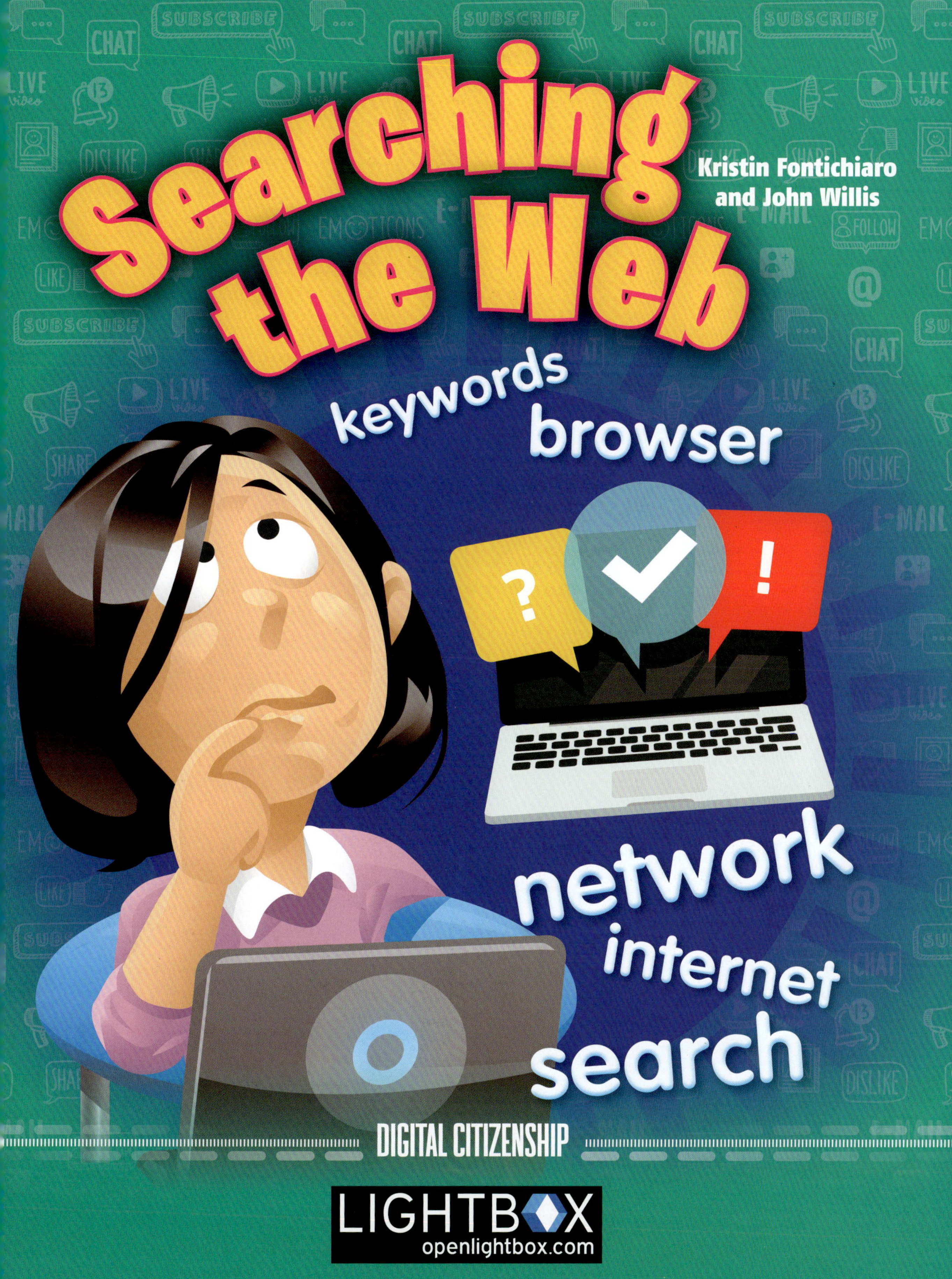
Searching the Web
Kristin Fontichiaro
and John Willis
keywords
browser
network
internet
search
DIGITAL CITIZENSHIP
LIGHTBOX
openlightbox.com

Go to **www.openlightbox.com** and enter this book's unique code.

ACCESS CODE

LBXG2927

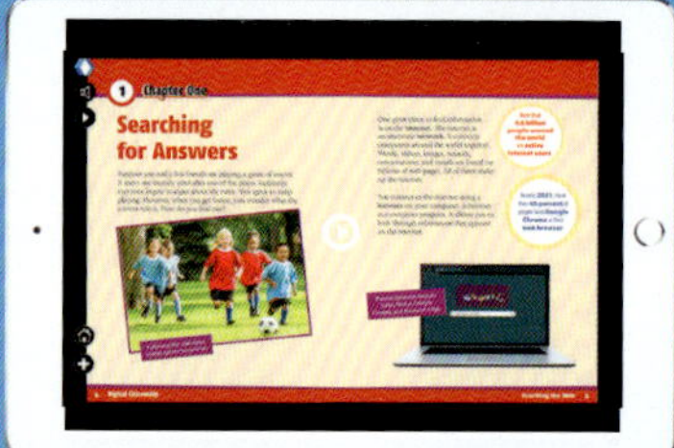

Lightbox is an all-inclusive digital solution for the teaching and learning of curriculum topics in an original, groundbreaking way. Lightbox is based on National Curriculum Standards.

LIGHTBOX SUPPLEMENTARY RESOURCES

SHARE
Share titles within your Learning Management System (LMS) or Library Circulation System

CURRICULUM
Find national and state curriculum correlations

CITATION
Create bibliographical references following the Chicago Manual of Style

STANDARD FEATURES OF LIGHTBOX

AUDIO High-quality narration using text-to-speech system

ACTIVITIES Printable PDFs that can be emailed and graded

SLIDESHOWS Pictorial overviews of key concepts

VIDEOS Embedded high-definition video clips

WEBLINKS Curated links to external, child-safe resources

TRANSPARENCIES Step-by-step layering of maps, diagrams, charts, and timelines

INTERACTIVE MAPS Interactive maps and aerial satellite imagery

QUIZZES Ten multiple-choice questions that are automatically graded and emailed for teacher assessment

KEY WORDS Matching key concepts to their definitions

This title is part of our Lightbox digital subscription

Lightbox Grades 3–5 Subscription
ISBN 978-1-5105-5424-5

Access hundreds of Lightbox titles with our digital subscription. Sign up for a **FREE** subscription trial at **www.openlightbox.com/trial**

Contents

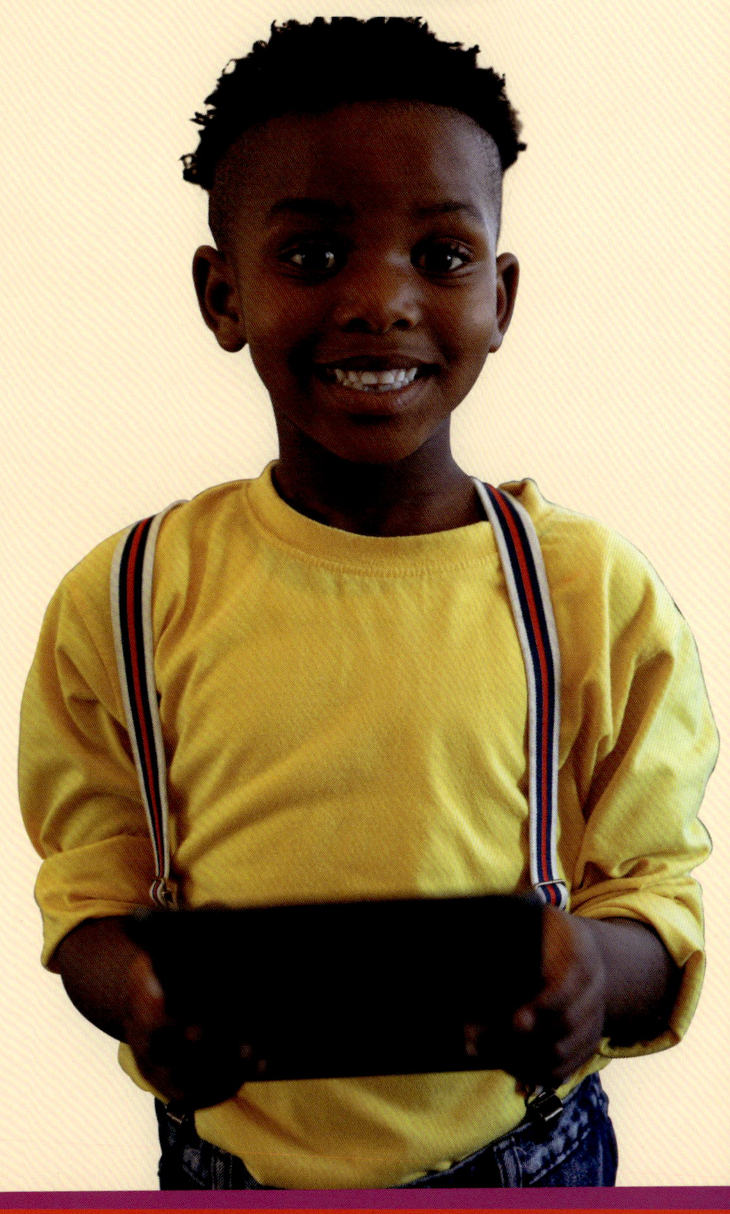

1 Chapter One

Searching for Answers

Suppose you and a few friends are playing a game of soccer. It starts out friendly until after one of the plays. Suddenly, everyone begins to argue about the rules. You agree to keep playing. However, when you get home, you wonder what the correct rule is. How do you find out?

Following the rules helps to keep games fun and fair.

One great place to find information is on the **internet**. The internet is an electronic **network**. It connects computers around the world together. Words, videos, images, sounds, conversations, and emails are found on billions of web pages. All of them make up the internet.

You connect to the internet using a **browser** on your computer. A browser is a computer program. It allows you to look through information that appears on the internet.

More than **4.6 billion people around the world** are **active internet users**.

In early **2021**, more than **65 percent** of people used **Google Chrome** as their **web browser**.

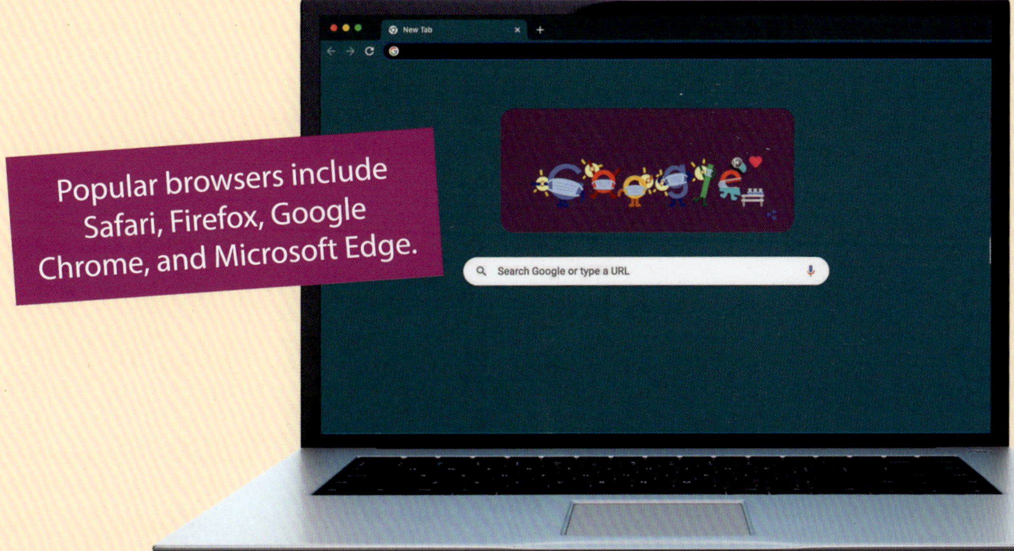

Popular browsers include Safari, Firefox, Google Chrome, and Microsoft Edge.

Once you are online, you can use a **search engine**. It looks for the information you request. Some good search engines for kids are:

www.kiddle.co
www.safesearchkids.com
www.wackysafe.com

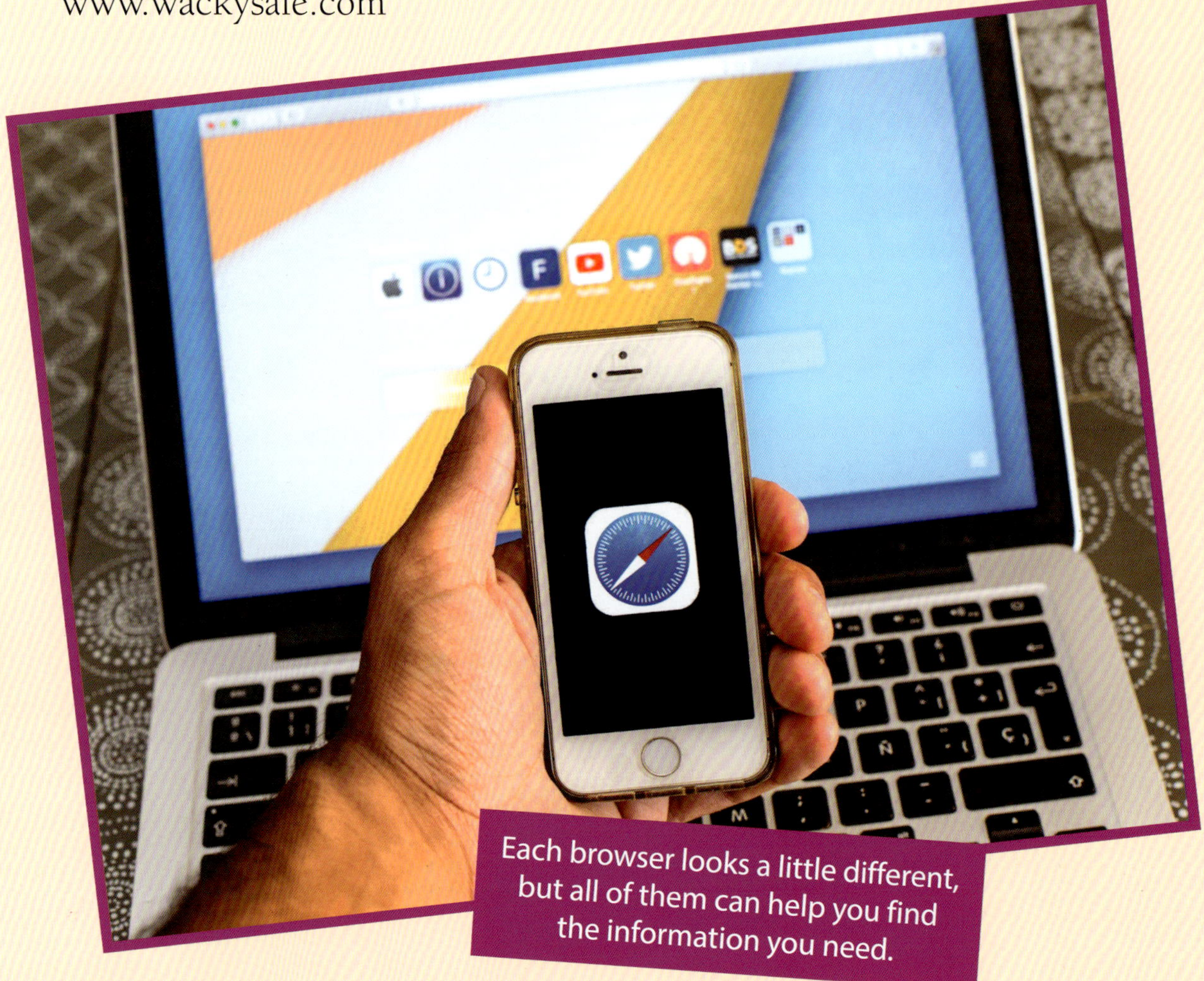

Each browser looks a little different, but all of them can help you find the information you need.

Try This

Open a search engine on a computer at home or at school. If you need help, ask your teacher or librarian. Type in the words *soccer rules*. Then press Return or Enter on your keyboard.

How many results did you get? What kind of information about soccer rules did you find?

History of Web Browsers

1993
Mosaic, a browser which displays both text and images, is introduced.

1995
Internet Explorer becomes the default web browser for computers using the Windows operating system.

2003
Safari is released as the default browser for Apple devices.

2008
Google launches its Chrome browser.

2013
Chrome becomes the world's most popular internet browser.

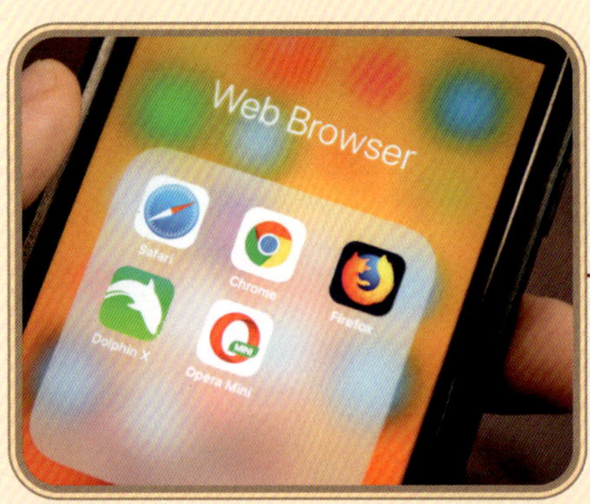

2021
Mobile web browsers grow in popularity as more than 50 percent of internet traffic comes from mobile devices.

Mapping Web Browsers

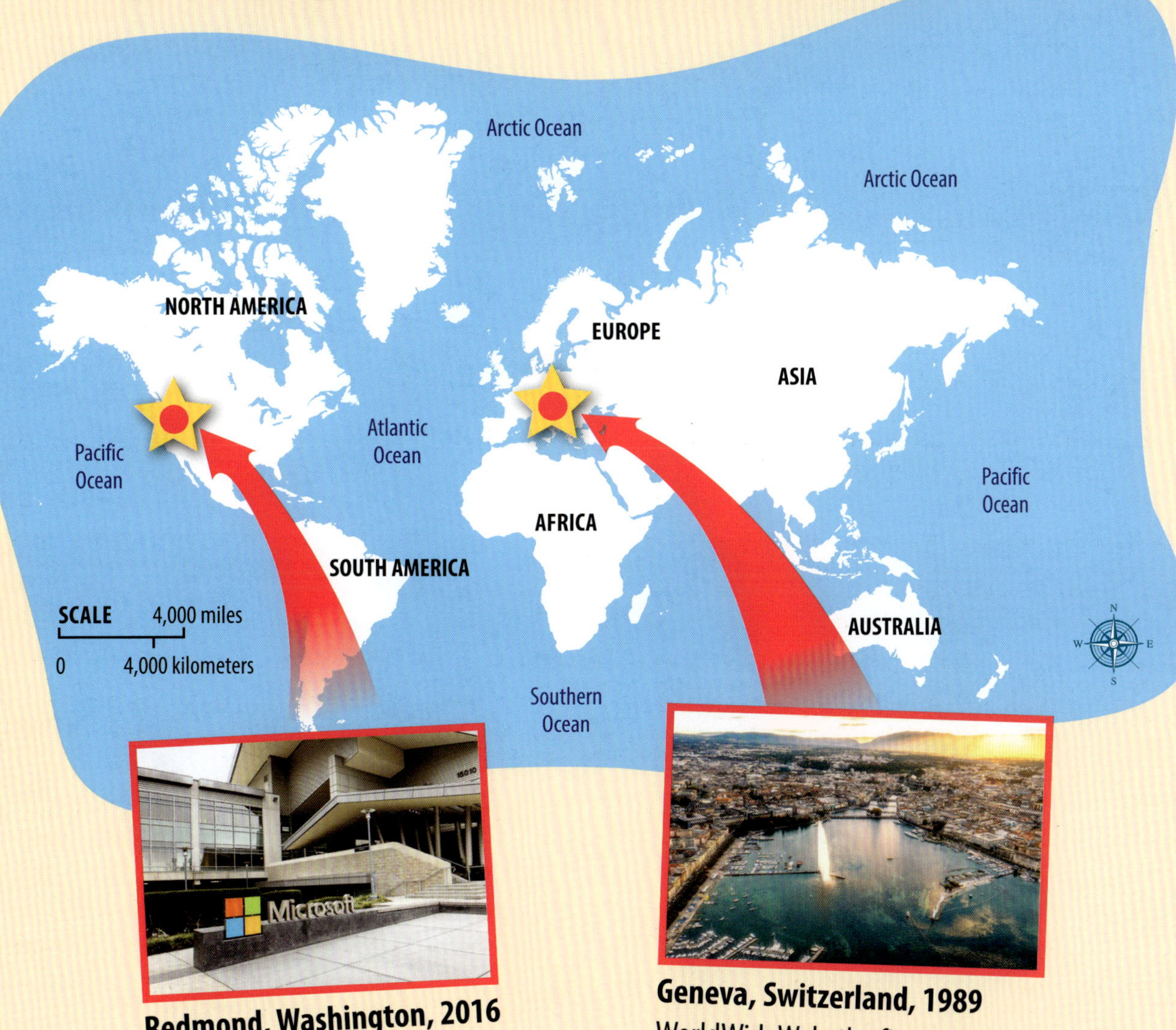

Redmond, Washington, 2016
Microsoft replaces Internet Explorer with the more secure Edge browser.

Geneva, Switzerland, 1989
WorldWideWeb, the first web browser, is developed by British scientist Tim Berners-Lee.

2 Chapter Two

Keywords

Your search for soccer rules probably produced thousands of web pages. Maybe even millions of pages! What if you spent just one second looking at each page? It would take you months to see them all.

Developing strategies can help make any task simpler or faster.

Choosing good keywords makes it easy to find particular information you are looking for.

There are so many choices. How do you find the information you need? You use strategies. A strategy is a tool or clever plan that helps you reach your goal.

When we look for information online, we are searching. Smart searchers think about the words that describe what they are looking for. We call these words **keywords**. Usually, they are nouns. Nouns are the names of people, places, or things.

Say you want to find out the size of a baseball. Your question is, "How big is a baseball?" There are two main ideas in that question. One is size. *Big* is an **adjective**. For your search, use the noun *size*. The other idea is baseball. Go to your search engine's search box. Type in *size baseball*.

Maybe your question is, "What kind of pet is best for my family?" Great keywords are *family pet*, *household pet*, and *safe pet*.

Skip short, common words in your search. You do not need to type in *is*, *the*, *a*, *for*, *of*, or *my*. You can skip capital letters and punctuation, but you need to spell carefully. A friend or grown-up can help.

Search engines typically look for variations of words. If you search for *pet*, you will also get results for *pets*.

Try This

Practice turning these questions into keywords:

- When is the next full Moon?
- How old is the president?
- How do you play basketball?
- What is the distance between New York City, New York, and Los Angeles, California?

1. Open a blank page in your notebook. Use a ruler to draw a line down the center of the page. You should now have two long boxes.

2. Write "Question" at the top of the box on the left. Write the four questions from the list above in this box.

3. Write "Keywords" at the top of the box on the right. Write the names of the keywords you would use to search for answers to the questions.

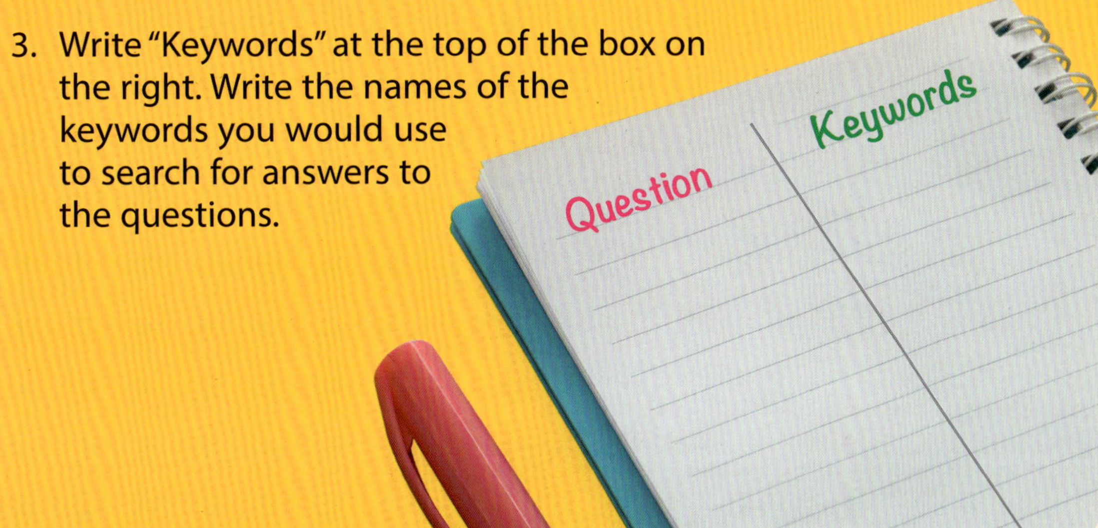

3 Chapter Three

Understanding Results

It only takes a second to get the results of a search. A list of web pages will appear on your computer screen. Each item in the list is called a **hit**.

Remember your search for soccer rules? Go back and look at the results.

Google is the most popular search engine used today.

Some words appear blue. These words are called **hyperlinks**, or links. Click on the link. You will be taken to that web page.

Below each hyperlink are a few words called a **snippet**. A snippet briefly tells you what is on that page. Read the snippets to see if a page seems useful and easy to read. Many websites were made for adults. These snippets might be hard to read. If so, click on another result.

A website's address is also known as its uniform resource locator, or URL.

Are you using Google or Bing as your search engine? Images or videos about your subject might come up. Do your search. Then, click on "Images" or "Videos."

Many browsers guess which websites will help you the most. They list these sites at the top of your results. Some hits may not be helpful. That is because a machine made the list for you. A person might have made a different list.

Keep a list of the websites you use for a project. It is how you show where you found the information. You will be able to find it again, too. Write or type out the website's address (such as *www.whitehouse.gov*) on a piece of paper or in a computer document. Do not write the address of the search engine.

Try This

Look through the first few pages of your search results for *soccer rules.*

- Which three sites look the most helpful? Why?
- Which three look the least helpful? Why?

1. Take two sheets of paper from your notebook.

2. On the first sheet, use a ruler to draw a line down the center of the page. You should now have two long boxes. Write "Most Helpful" at the top of the column on the left. Write "Reasons Why" at the top of the column on the right.

3. On the second sheet, draw a line down the center of the page. Write "Least Helpful" at the top of the column on the left. Write "Reasons Why" at the top of the column on the right.

4. Then, write your answers to the questions.

4 Chapter Four

Narrowing Your Search

Roberto loves football, especially the Buffalo Bills. He wants to learn more about his favorite team. He types in the keywords *buffalo* and *bills*. Some results are about the football team. However, some are about animals called buffalo, a man named Buffalo Bill, or a buffalo nickel.

How can Roberto just get results about the football team? He needs to narrow his search. That way, he will get fewer hits. Roberto can add quotation marks around the words "buffalo bills." This tells the search engine to list certain web pages. Those pages have the word *buffalo* next to the word *bills*. Websites about buffalo nickels will not show up. Buffalo Bill the man will not, either. Why? Because the search is for *bills*, not *bill*.

Using a minus sign can tell a search engine not to look for a word.

Try This

If you search for "*george washington*," which of these snippets might show up?

a. George Washington was the first president of the United States.
b. George visited Washington, D.C., this summer.
c. George Smith and Mary Washington were married.
d. Our neighbor, Mrs. George, moved to Seattle, Washington.

Did you guess "a"? You are right! The other results do not have *george* and *washington* right next to each other.

5 Chapter Five

Subject Directories

A **subject directory** is another good tool. It can help you find information on the internet. Subject directories are collections of websites gathered and organized by people. They start with a few main categories. Then, they branch out into **subtopics**.

Suppose you wanted to find information about black bear cubs. Go to a subject directory. Start by clicking on *mammals*. Then, click on *bears*. Next, try *black bears*. You narrow your subject each time you click on a subtopic. This strategy is called "drilling down."

Most libraries offer useful subject directories that you can use for free.

What if you drill down and do not find any information? Back up! Try another path. Most subject directories also have a search box.

Try This

Ask your teacher or librarian to show you one of these subject directories:

1. KidSpace at the Internet Public Library (www.ipl.org/div/kidspace)
2. National Geographic Kids (https://kids.nationalgeographic.com/animals/)
3. SIRS Discoverer database (ask a librarian)
4. PebbleGo database (ask a librarian)

Do you like subject directories? Or do you like typing in keywords more? How are they different?

Quiz

1
When was the Mosaic web browser introduced?

2
What does a browser allow people to do?

3
What is another name for a website's address?

4
What is a minus sign used for when searching?

5
Who developed WorldWideWeb?

6
Which words are blue in search results?

7
What are subject directories?

8
What is the default browser for Apple devices?

9
What kind of words are often keywords?

10
How many people around the world are active internet users?

Answers: 1. 1993 **2.** Look through information that appears on the internet **3.** Uniform resource locator, or URL **4.** To tell a search engine not to look for a word **5.** Tim Berners-Lee **6.** Hyperlinks, or links **7.** Collections of websites gathered and organized by people **8.** Safari **9.** Nouns **10.** More than 4.6 billion

Key Words

adjective: a word that describes a noun or a pronoun

browser: a computer program that lets you find and look through web pages or other data

hit: a website that is displayed as the result of a search

hyperlinks: references to web pages that the reader can directly follow to the web pages by clicking on them

internet: the electronic network that allows millions of computers around the world to connect together

keywords: words or phrases used to describe the contents of a document

network: a system of things that are connected to each other

search engine: a computer program that will help you find information you request

snippet: words that appear in search results and describe a website

subject directory: a collection of websites gathered and organized by people, not computers

subtopics: specific topics in a subject directory

Index

LIGHTBOX

SUPPLEMENTARY RESOURCES

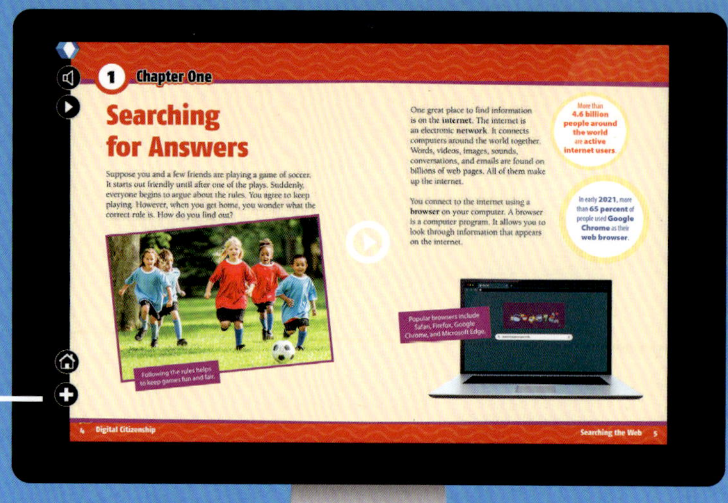

Click on the plus icon found in the bottom left corner of each spread to open additional teacher resources.

- Download and print the book's quizzes and activities
- Access curriculum correlations
- Explore additional web applications that enhance the Lightbox experience

LIGHTBOX DIGITAL TITLES
Packed full of integrated media

VIDEOS

INTERACTIVE MAPS

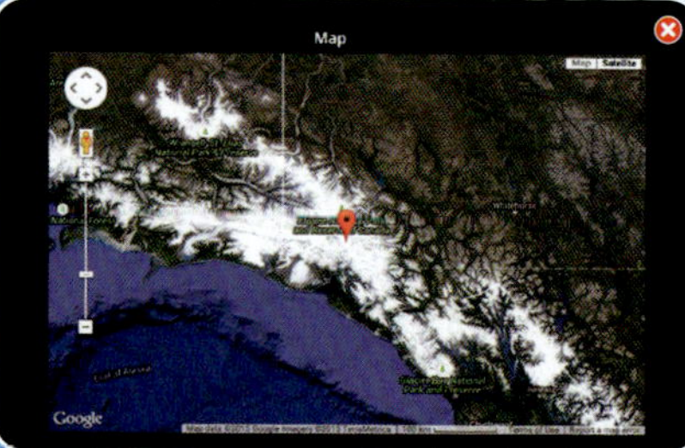

WEBLINKS

SLIDESHOWS

QUIZZES

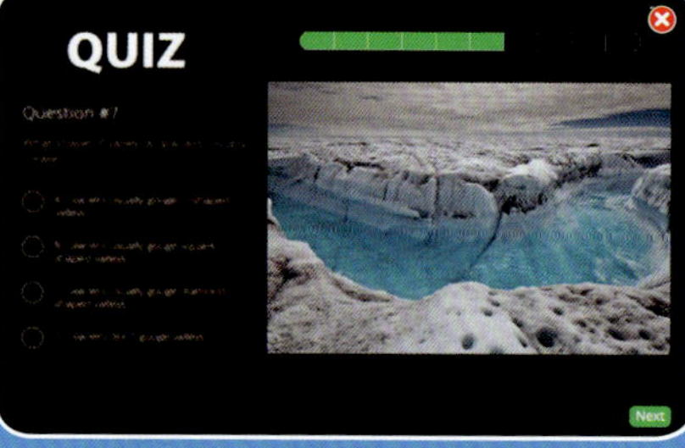

OPTIMIZED FOR
- ✓ TABLETS
- ✓ WHITEBOARDS
- ✓ COMPUTERS
- ✓ AND MUCH MORE!

Published by Lightbox Learning
276 5th Avenue
Suite 704 #917
New York, NY 10001
Website: www.openlightbox.com

Copyright ©2022 Lightbox Learning
All rights reserved. No part of this publication may be reproduced, stored in a retrieval system, or transmitted in any form or by any means, electronic, mechanical, photocopying, recording, or otherwise, without the prior written permission of the publisher.

First published by Cherry Lake Publishing in 2012

Library of Congress Control Number: 2021939446

ISBN 978-1-5105-5562-4 (hardcover)
ISBN 978-1-5105-5563-1 (multi-user eBook)

Printed in Guangzhou, China
1 2 3 4 5 6 7 8 9 0 25 24 23 22 21

082021
111020

Project Coordinator John Willis
Designer Jean Faye Marie Rodriguez

Photo Credits
Every reasonable effort has been made to trace ownership and to obtain permission to reprint copyright material. The publisher would be pleased to have any errors or omissions brought to its attention so that they may be corrected in subsequent printings.

The publisher acknowledges Getty Images as its primary image supplier for this title.